Kibby®
the Space Dog

by Andrea Cassell   illustrated by Melanie Regier Koop

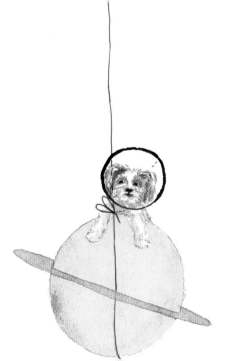
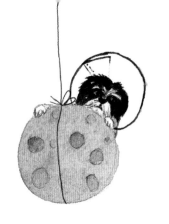

To my children
and grandchildren ...
I love you
to the moon and back.

Kibby the Space Dog

Cover design by Melanie Regier Koop
Book design and layout by Melanie Regier Koop

For more information, please contact:
Mascot Books
620 Herndon Parkway, Suite 320
Herndon, VA 20170
info@mascotbooks.com

Library of Congress Control Number: 2019917454

CPSIA Code: PRT0120A
ISBN-13: 978-1-64543-340-8

Printed in the United States

KIBBY is an ordinary, adorable dog that experienced something we all experience at one point in our lives...Rejection.

Along his journey he discovered things that will inspire children to accept who they are and accept others who are different. He learned the importance of not judging others for the way they look. When Kibby had to wear "the cone of shame," due to stitches, he truly experienced rejection. Children were reluctant to touch or get near him. During his walks, other dogs on the street ignored him. He was an unhappy dog and really disliked wearing the cone!

Kibby's real life experience inspired me to write this beautifully illustrated picture book. Even though Kibby is a dog, he feels and thinks just like we do. I want to convey the message to children, that it's okay to be different! My hope is that children celebrate similarities in each other, rather than notice the differences.

Celebrate being unique!
With Kibby Kisses, X X
Andrea

My name is **Kibby.**

I'm a miniature labradoodle.

I was born on St. Patrick's Day.

Life is wonderful!

I'm a
happy dog!

sniff
sniff
sniff

I love taking big, adventurous walks in
my neighborhood. I watch the squirrels run
around me. I listen to the birds chirping.
I let other dogs sniff me.

I am good friends with the dogs in my neighborhood. They give me lots of kisses.

Car rides are a special treat.

I get to stick my head out. I can see everything
around me. I love the wind in my face.

People in other cars smile and wave at me.
They say, "What a cute dog!"

The children
in my neighborhood
play games with me.

I love it!

I am a happy dog!

I kiss
all the
kids!

One day, I had to visit the doctor at the veterinary clinic. I really liked the vet, especially because I got some yummy treats! I saved up lots of kisses for the doctor too!

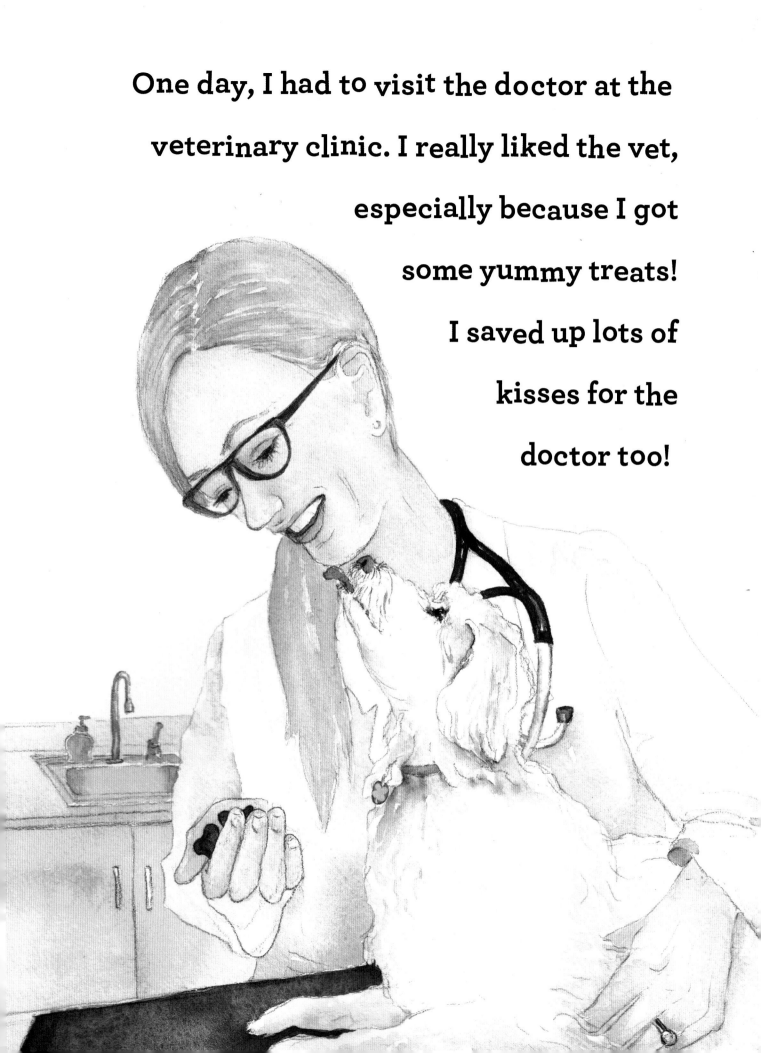

I needed stitches for a small cut
on one of my paws.

The doctor put a plastic cone-shaped
object around my head, so I wouldn't
chew on my stitches.

I didn't like the plastic cone!

It was different.

It bothered me.

I was a sad dog!

When I got home, I tried to
eat, drink, sleep, and play with my toys,
but it was so very hard to do anything
with that darn plastic cone
around my head!

I had to keep

the plastic cone

on my head

for 2 weeks!

It was a really long time.

I was a sad dog!

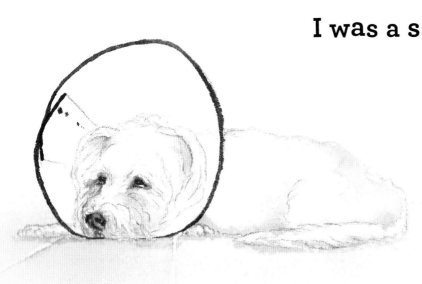

For some reason, my big, adventurous walks were not the same.

The squirrels ignored me, the birds didn't chirp and the dogs didn't sniff me anymore.

And I didn't get any kisses.

My car rides were not the same, either.

People in other cars laughed at me.

They said, "Look at that dog!"

The children in my neighborhood didn't want to play games with me! I think they were afraid of me. I was a sad dog!

I couldn't do any of the
fun things I used to do.
Life wasn't so wonderful!

I was being rejected

because people thought I was different now.

My life was not the same anymore.

I lost my fun,

playful spirit.

One night...

I had this amazing dream!

I went to outer space. I saw

lots of dogs wearing plastic

cones on their heads just like

me! I saw many kinds of dogs.

Big
and
LITTLE
dogs.

The dogs were happy!

And I didn't stand out.

I wasn't the only one who had a

plastic cone around his head!

Outer space was fun!

No one judged me or laughed at me.

All the dogs treated me the same.

I got lots of **sniff** sniff sniffs

I watched other
dogs and learned to eat,
drink, sleep and play
with the plastic cone
around my head.

I was a happy dog!

All of a sudden...

I woke up.

I found myself back in my bed.

It was only a dream.

I was a sad dog!

Again!

I wanted to be back in space with the

other dogs, who were just like me.

No one would ignore me.

And no one would laugh at me.

And everyone would play games with me.

And everyone would

sniff

sniff

sniff

me!

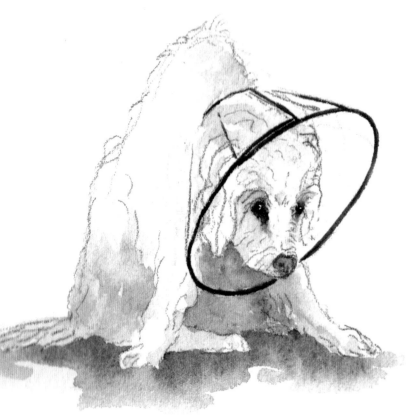

These past 2 weeks

were hard for me.

It seemed like years.

I got used to the

way things were.

I accepted it.

Today, I went to
visit my doctor again.
She checked
the stitches to see
if my paw had healed.

The doctor said that I had healed nicely.
She said the plastic cone could come off. Yippie!
I was a happy dog!

When I got home,
I went for more big,
adventurous walks
in my neighborhood.

sniff
sniff
sniff

The squirrels
ran around me,
the birds were chirping
and the dogs sniffed me.

I went for a ride in the car.
I stuck my head out so I could see
everything around me.

People in other cars smiled at me
and said, "What a cute dog!"

The children in my neighborhood played games with me!

And I was so delighted. I was a happy dog! I loved and kissed everyone!

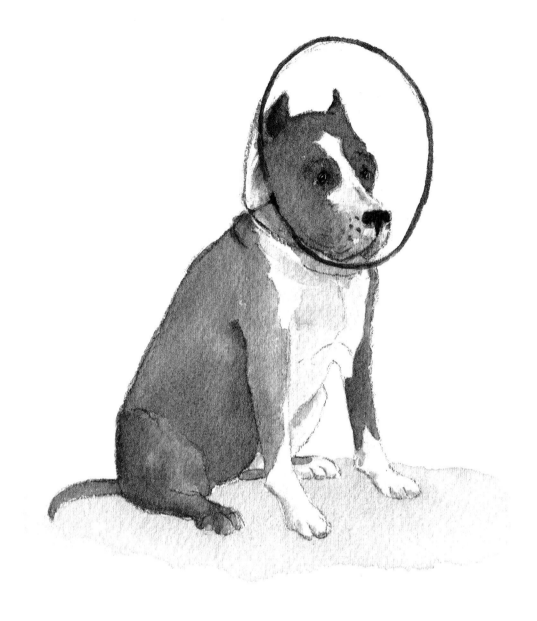

One day, on one of my adventurous walks,
I saw a dog in my neighborhood wearing a
plastic cone around his head.

He looked like a sad dog!

So, I went over to the dog.

I gave him a nice  **sniff** sniff sniff

He was very friendly.

He gave lots of kisses too.

I remembered how I felt when

I had the plastic cone

around my head.

I remembered how everyone

ignored me. I remembered

how I didn't fit in.

I remembered how I was a sad dog!

And I didn't want this dog to feel

the same way I did.

I hoped the dog would have an

amazing dream, like me.

I hoped he would dream he saw

lots of dogs in space,

wearing plastic cones on their

heads, just like him!

And no one would judge him.

And no one would laugh at him.

And he would be in a wonderful place

where everyone was treated the same.

And then he would be

a happy dog!

Flip this page to see real photos of Kibby and his friends!